The King of the Snakes and Other Folk-Lore Stories from Uganda

Mrs. George Baskerville

Illustrated by Mrs. E. G. Morris

THE KING OF THE SNAKES

AND OTHER FOLK-LORE STORIES
FROM UGANDA

BY
MRS. GEORGE BASKERVILLE

ILLUSTRATED BY MRS. E. G. MORRIS

DEDICATED TO
ALL THE LITTLE CHILDREN
I LOVED IN UGANDA

First published 1922.

THE KING OF THE SNAKES

OF THE

SNAKES

BY
ROSETTA BASKERVILLE

PREFACE

I AM indebted to SIR APOLO KAGWA, K.C.M.G., M.B.E., KATIKIRO OF BUGANDA, for some of the stories in this book, for I first read them in his "Engero za Baganda," a little work in the Luganda language, now unfortunately out of print.

The rest is a small selection from a large number I have picked up during some years in the country–from old wives sitting over their cooking-pots in smoky kitchens, from porters round the camp fire at night, and from that charming mixed multitude which made up "the good old days."

ROSETTA BASKERVILLE.

NAMBI AND HER BROTHERS VISIT

KINTU, who LIVED ALONE with his cow

CONTENTS

LIST OF ILLUSTRATIONS

THE KING OF THE SNAKES

THERE is a beautiful village near the Great Lake, called Kalungu. The houses nestle into the banana gardens, and there are sunny little courtyards with lemon and guava trees and pawpaw-trees heavy with fruit. The little boys who herd the goats on the hill-sides have no fear, for everything is peaceful and happy.

But once upon a time Kalungu was a very sorrowful place, for a big snake called Sesota lived on the hill-side and came down every day to the village and caught people and ate them.

Every day this happened, until the people ran away to other villages, and Kalungu was left desolate and empty.

The King heard of this, and he asked in the Council what could be done to kill Sesota, and one chief said one thing and another chief said another, but no one was found brave enough to go to Kalungu and kill the great snake.

Then a poor peasant man, called Waswa, came to the Council and said: "Sirs, I will kill Sesota"; and they offered him spears and big hunting knives, but he refused them all and said: "Give me a large water-pot and some blue beads and some brass and ivory bracelets and a ring, and I will go and kill Sesota."

So they gave him all he asked, and he set out on his journey, his little son carrying the water-pot with the other things inside it; and as he walked he played this tune on his reed pipe:

> Sesota, Sesota, King of the Snakes,
>   Beautiful presents I bring.
> The King of Uganda has sent me to-day
>   With bracelets and beads and a ring.

The King of the Snakes

As he neared Kalungu the old snake on the hillside heard him corning, and because snakes are very fond of music he listened gladly and sang back:

> I am Sesota, the King of the Snakes;
>   Two bold intruders I see.
> But if they bring me the gifts of a King
>   They will be welcomed by me.

So Waswa and his little son entered the village and sat down in the courtyard of a deserted house, and the child put down the water-pot and then hid in the house, and Waswa played his pipe, all the time the same tune.

Very soon he heard the great snake rustling down the hill-side and along the village road till it came to the courtyard where Waswa sat; he never stopped playing until the snake went up to the water-pot and looked in to see his presents. Then Waswa sang this song:

> Sesota, Sesota, King of the Snakes,
>   Enter this water-pot here.
> The King of Uganda has sent you a bed
>   On which you shall sleep for a year.

When the great snake heard this song he got into the water-pot and coiled himself round and settled down to sleep, and Waswa played very softly over and over again:

> *Sesota, Sesota, Sesota, Sesota, Sesota, Sesota, Sesota.*

When he saw that the great snake was sound asleep he called softly to his son, and the child came very quietly and put the lid on the water-pot and tied it tightly down, and they picked it up and went on their way back to the capital, and Waswa played all the way on his pipe and sang this song:

> Sesota, Sesota, King of the Snakes,
>   Sleeps on the bed of a King.

The King of the Snakes

> Beat all the drums, play all the harps,
> Dance and make merry and sing.

And every village they came to the people ran out after them, singing and dancing and beating drums and playing harps because the great snake who had eaten so many people had been caught, and the crowd increased more and more until they arrived in the capital, and the King and his chiefs came out of the Council House, and there was great rejoicing.

And the King commanded the people to make a bonfire, and they burnt Sesota the great snake.

Then the King said to Waswa: "I will give you the village of Kalungu, and you shall be chief of that place, you and your children after you, and they shall be called 'Wakalungu.'" And his little boy, who had carried the water-pot, was chief after him, and his grandchildren live in Kalungu to-day, and if you go there you will see them, and perhaps they will tell you about Sesota.

THE STORY OF KINTU

ONCE upon a time, a very long while ago, there were no people in the country of Uganda except one man, and his name was Kintu. He had one cow, and this cow was his great friend, but he was very lonely all by himself on the Earth.

Now up in the sky there was a lovely kingdom called the Cloud Land, and the King was called Gulu. He had many sons and daughters, and these children used to wait for a rainbow to touch the Earth, and then they would slide down it and stay a little while below, playing among the trees; but they couldn't stay long, for a rainbow very soon melts away in the hot Sun, and if they had waited too long they could not have climbed home to the Cloud Land. One day two of Gulu's sons saw a rainbow touching the Earth, and they called to their sister Nambi to come with them. Nambi was a very beautiful girl, and the King Gulu loved her very much. She went quickly with her brothers and slid down to the Earth, and the part of the Earth the rainbow touched was Uganda, and there they saw Kintu sitting all alone watching his cow graze. At first they were rather frightened, for they had never seen a man before, but they soon made friends with Kintu, and they stayed a long time talking to him. He told them how lonely he was, and Nambi, who had a tender heart, was very sorry for him, and she said: "I will come back again and marry you, and then you won't be lonely any more in this beautiful country." When they were on their way home the brothers reproved Nambi; they said: "Why did you say that? You know our father Gulu will never allow you to go away and marry Kintu."

But Nambi said: "I *will* go, I promised Kintu, and my father would never wish me to break my promise. I will go home now and tell my father, and then pack up all my things, and go to the Earth to live there always."

When they arrived back in the Cloud Land they told Gulu all they had done, and Nambi told him that she had promised to marry Kintu, and go and live on the Earth. At first Gulu was angry, but at last he gave his consent, but on one condition. He said to Nambi: "If you want to be happy on the Earth you must go secretly; pack your things very carefully, and these two brothers will go with you and see that you arrive safely; but, whatever you do, you must not tell any of the others that you are going. If your brother Death, whom we call Walumbe, hears of it, he will want to go with you, and he will spoil your beautiful Earth."

So Nambi and her two brothers packed all her things in bundles, and she said good-bye to her father, and they started down a rainbow. Suddenly Nambi stopped. "Oh, I have forgotten the millet seed for my fowls," she said, "and as Kintu has no fowls he will have no millet seed, and my fowls will die; I must hurry back and fetch it." She went back quickly and found the little parcel of seeds, and just as she was starting for the rainbow again she met her brother Walumbe. "Where are you going?" he asked. Nambi was very frightened, and at first she would not tell him, but Walumbe would not go away. "Where you go I am going too," he said.

"You cannot come with me," cried poor Nambi. "I am going to the Earth, and our father said you were not to go with me."

"Oh, ho!" said Walumbe, "so you have tried to have a secret from me; well, you can go off, but I shall come and visit you and your man Kintu very soon."

Poor Nambi cried very much, and when she came to the place where her brothers were waiting for her she told them. They were horrified and afraid what their father Gulu might say, and they said to Nambi, "If you had not been disobedient this would not have happened"; but as nothing could be done they all slid down the rainbow to the Earth, and Nambi soon forgot her tears when she met Kintu again and saw how happy she had made him by coming back

Then the brothers said good-bye to her and went home, and Nambi began to make her new life. She untied the bundle of banana stalks and showed Kintu how to plant them in rows wide apart, for she said: "They will spread and need room to grow"; then she planted a barkcloth branch from which in time she showed Kintu how to make barkcloth, and she sowed some of the millet seed, so that her fowls should always have food; and she and Kintu were very busy and very happy and loved each other very much.

Then one day Walumbe came down to see them, and Nambi was very frightened. She told Kintu all about him and said: "We must get rid of him at all costs; my father Gulu told me he would spoil our happiness." But nothing would induce Walumbe to go away, and at last Kintu promised him: "If you will go away, not to return, I will give you my first child"; and then he went back. Kintu and Nambi lived many years happily together and had many sons and daughters, and Kintu forgot all about his promise. At last, one day, Walumbe came back and claimed his child. Kintu was very angry and tried to drive him away, but this time Walumbe would not go, and he said, "As you did not keep your promise and give me your first child, now I will stay on the Earth always, and I will take what I want." And although Kintu and Nambi had so many children and grandchildren and great-grandchildren that Uganda was soon full of people, still every now and then cruel Walumbe came and took one away, sometimes an old man and sometimes a young one and sometimes a little baby. But still the country of Uganda is full of people who have beautiful banana gardens, and many cows and fowls, and little fat children with skins like chocolate, and the rainbows still come down from the Cloud Land and touch the Earth, as they did in the days when Nambi played with her brothers.

THE STORY OF THE FAIRY BEE

BEFORE Nambi came to live on the Earth, when Kintu was quite alone, he made friends with a bumble-bee. There had been a great rainstorm, and the poor bee fell to the ground on his back and could not get up again, and the heavy raindrops beat on him and very soon he would have died of cold, but Kintu picked him up and held him in his warm hand, and soon the bumble-bee revived and said to Kintu: "You have saved my life; I will always be your friend and help you when you are in trouble."

One morning he woke up and found that his cow was gone; he could not find it anywhere. Then the bumble-bee came to him and said: "I will help you find your cow; it has been stolen by the herdsmen of a wizard who lives on the Mountains of the Moon." So Kintu took his stick and set out on his long journey to the far-away mountains where the snow never melts, and the bumble-bee flew before him to show him the way. On they went, day after day, through dark forests and over wide rivers, and by narrow paths through the jungle grass, until they saw the Mountains of the Moon in the far distance. Then the bumble-bee said: "Do everything that I tell you, for you will never be able to outwit the old wizard and his people by yourself, and if you do not prove yourself cleverer than they are, they will never give you back your cow." When they arrived in the wizard's country and the great mountains were towering above them, Kintu saw what a rich country it was–great herds of cattle and flocks of sheep and goats, and beautiful gardens, and many people. When the wizard heard that Kintu had arrived, he sent for him and said: "Are you really Kintu, the man who lives all alone with a cow?" And Kintu said: "Yes, I am, and your people have stolen my cow, and I have come to find it." Then the wizard wondered very much, and said to his people: "This is a very wonderful man; we will see what marvels he can do. How did he find his way from Uganda, and how did he know that you stole his cow while he was asleep, for there was no one to tell him? We will test him and see if he is really a wise man." So they gave him a house to rest in, and said they would bring him some supper. Kintu rested a little while, and then to his surprise, ten thousand people arrived, each carrying a basket of cooked food.

"The wizard has sent you your supper," they said, and put down the ten thousand baskets. "Thank them very much," whispered the bee in Kintu's ear, "and tell them to come back in a little while and fetch their baskets when you have finished your supper." So the people went away wondering very much. "Is it possible for one man to eat so much?" Then the bee called all the ants in the country: the red ants which live in the forests and are always hungry, for they can eat a dead elephant if they find it; and the white ants who build big castles for themselves of red earth which look like huts on the hill-sides, and in the middle of the castle is a beautiful room with smooth walls where their Queen lives; and the large black ants which run very fast and lose their way every two minutes and run back again to find it; and the little black ants who are always silently watching everywhere, though one does not see them, and run out quickly to pick up a crumb or a seed or a grain of corn directly they see it on the ground. All these came, millions, and millions, and millions of them, and they carried away the food, until the baskets were all empty except one, which Kintu ate for his supper. Then the people came back, and they shouted when they saw the empty baskets piled up together. "Can one man eat so much? This man is a wizard."

When the old wizard heard it he said: "Let him sleep, to-morrow we will give him another test." In the morning they brought him a brass axe and said: "Our chief likes rocks for his fire; go and cut firewood from the rocks and bring it tied up in bundles." Then the bee flew before him as he climbed up the mountain-side and brought him to a rock that had been struck all into splinters by lightning, and he tied the splinters together with grass and returned, and all the people wondered very much, and said: "This must be Kintu, the man who lives by himself."

Then they brought him a water-pot and said: "Our chief does not drink water, he only drinks dew. Go and fill this pot in the forest." So Kintu climbed up the mountain, and this time the journey was very long; seven peaks they climbed and then they came to the bamboo forest. The bumble-bee flew before him and cheered him on and told the shivering bamboos who he was, and as he walked the bamboos whispered: "This is Kintu, let us help him; this is Kintu, this is Kintu."

Then the bumble-bee showed him a hole in a rock, and all the bamboos shook their branches at once, and the hole was filled with dew, and Kintu filled his water-pot and returned. Then the old wizard laughed and said: "You are a marvellous man, I will not tease you any more; if you can recognize your cow in my herd, you shall take it and go home to Uganda."

So all the herds were collected, and Kintu was told to find his cow, and the bumble-bee flew before him as he made his way between the cows–thousands and thousands of cows, with long horns all standing upright. Then the bumble-bee alighted on t;he horn of a cow, and Kintu saw it was his old friend, and he drove it out of the herd and showed it to the wizard and his people and said: "This is my cow that they stole from me while I slept," and he said good-bye to them, and the bumble-bee showed him the way home to Uganda.

And to-day if you go to the Mountains of the Moon and climb up to the bamboo forests, the trees will learn down to see you and whisper to each other: "This is Kintu, this is Kintu, this is Kintu!" for they remember the first man they ever saw, and think he has come back.

THE STORY OF MPOBE THE HUNTER

ONCE upon a time there lived a man called Mpobe; he was a hunter, and he had a dog which went hunting with him. The jungle is very thick in the Uganda forests, so Mpobe tied a little bell to his dog for fear he should lose it. When they had been hunting for some time, a little animal called a musu ran out of the jungle grass, and the dog gave chase, and Mpobe ran after the dog.

On they went through the jungle, and it seemed as if the musu would never be caught. At last it ran into a hole and the dog followed it, and when Mpobe came up he found the hole looked like the entrance to a tunnel, and, as he heard the dog's bell tinkling far away, he ran into the hole and followed it. On and on they went in the dark, down into the Earth, and Mpobe ran on because he still heard the bell, and he wanted to catch the musu. All hunters in every country are like this; they do not like to go home and say they have killed nothing.

Suddenly the tunnel came to an end, and Mpobe found himself in a country right down in the centre of the Earth. It was a beautiful country, with lovely gardens and trees and flowers and rivers, and flocks of sheep and goats and herds of cattle were grazing in the green fields. Still the musu ran on and the dog ran after it, and Mpobe followed them, looking from side to side as he ran, and wondering at all he saw. At last they came to a courtyard, and Mpobe followed them into it; the dog had not caught the musu. They were just resting quietly together in front of a very old man who sat all alone in the middle of the courtyard. Mpobe knelt down and greeted the old man, who said to him: "What are you doing here, and why have you come?"

"Sir," said Mpobe, "I do not know where I am. This is my dog, and we were hunting this musu above in the jungle, and the musu ran into a hole and my dog followed it, and I followed the dog, and we arrived here."

ᙏpoBe the ᙙunter

Then the old man said: "Do you know who I am? I am Walumbe, and when I go to the Earth and carry away people and cows and sheep and goats, I bring them all down here to my beautiful country of Death, but no one can go back again, and you and the musu and your dog must stay here for ever."

Then Mpobe cried bitterly and implored Walumbe to allow him to return. "I will not stay long," he said. "I will come back soon, just let me go and say good-bye to my friends."

Walumbe said: "I will let you go on one condition. You must tell nobody what you have seen or where you have been. If you will promise me to keep this secret, you may go back, but as sure as you tell it to anyone I will come for you, and then you must return here."

Mpobe promised gladly, and the old man showed him the way back. When he got home his mother and his wife and his relations rejoiced very much, because he had been away three days and they thought he was lost in the jungle, and they asked him where he had been and what he had seen, and to all he answered the same. "I was hunting a musu and I lost my way." This went on for many days, and he would tell them nothing, so they got tired of asking him; but one day he was alone in the house with his old mother and she asked him again: "Mpobe, my child, tell me what you saw in the jungle"; and he said: "I cannot tell you, I promised I would keep it quite secret "; and his mother said: "Whom did you promise, my child? Cannot you tell your old mother a little about it?"

Then Mpobe said: "Will you promise to tell no one if I tell you where I went and what I saw those three days in the jungle?" And the old woman said: "Whom should I tell, my child? Is not my heart yours?"

Then Mpobe told her all about his hunting and the musu and the tunnel, and the wonderful country in the middle of the Earth, and the very old man who was Walumbe.

That night, when everything was quiet and still, Mpobe heard a voice calling, "Mpobe! Mpobe!" And then he answered, and the voice said: "I am Walumbe; you have broken your promise, you must come with me, and this time there is no return." So they went away together into the jungle.

In the morning when his friends found that Mpobe was gone they wondered if he was hunting again, but his old mother told them the story, and they all went into the jungle and looked for the tunnel which leads to Walumbe's country, but though they searched for it and many other people have searched for it since then, no one has ever found it, and no one has ever seen Walumbe when he visits the Earth.

THE STORY OF WALUKAGA THE BLACKSMITH

A VERY long time ago there was a King in Uganda who was very cruel to his people, and they feared him very much. Every day he thought of new things to do which would distress and trouble them, until no man's life was safe, and no one was happy, and all through the beautiful country, although the Sun shone every day and the birds sang, sorrow and misery were in every village.

One day, the King sent for Walukaga, the chief of the blacksmiths, and said to him: "I want you to do a piece of work for me as you are such a clever man. I want you to make a man at your forge, not an iron man, but a real one with flesh and blood, one that can walk and talk and do everything that a real man does."

Walukaga bowed himself to the ground and went away very sad, for he saw that the King meant to kill him, for who but God can make a real man, and what blacksmith can make one at a forge? As he was going home, thinking sadly of these things, he met a madman, who greeted him with great joy. Now this man had been a very great friend of Walukaga's before he went mad, and the blacksmith had always been kind to him, so when he asked: "Why are you looking so sad?" Walukaga thought in his heart: "I have very few days to live; let me do a kindness while I can." So he took the madman aside and told him all the King had said.

The madman gave him some advice, and both of them went home. Walukaga thought over the madman's words and then he went back to the King and asked for an audience. When the King saw him he laughed and said: "Have you made the man yet at your forge?"

Then Walukaga said bravely: "Sir, I have thought about it, and I have come to ask your help because this is a very difficult task, and I cannot do it alone; a special kind of charcoal is needed, it is made of human hair, and I want three large sacks of it!"

Then the King gave the order, and messengers went through all the country ordering the people to shave their heads and send their hair to Walukaga. But when it was burnt there was not enough charcoal to fill one sack. Then Walukaga went again to the King and said: "Sir, before I can forge a man I must have water. But ordinary water will not do. I must have tears of men and women, for it takes many tears to make one human life. I want three water-pots full."

Then the King sent messengers all through the country ordering the men and women to keep their tears, and send them to Walukaga the blacksmith, but though the land was full of sorrow and the people wept every day, there were only enough tears to fill one water-pot. Then Walukaga went to the King and bowed very low, and knelt before him and fell on his face and said: "Sir, you set me a hard task to do, and I asked you to help me in an easy way. If a great King cannot do a small thing, how shall a poor blacksmith do the work of the Creator?"

Then the King said: "Walukaga is right. The thing I gave him to do was impossible," and he gave him a present and sent him away, and now in Uganda when a man is perplexed and does not know what to do in a great difficulty, his friends say: "Find a madman and ask his advice," because this has become a proverb since the days of Walukaga the blacksmith.

WHY THE BAT SLEEPS ALL THROUGH THE DAY AND ONLY GOES OUT AT NIGHT

AFTER Nambi had gone to live on the Earth her father Gulu, the King of the Cloud Land, called a great council together, and gave presents to all his friends.

Those who lived far away were called by special messengers, and he sent the Bat to call the Sun, and the Dove to call the Moon. The Dove is a sweet obedient creature, and it flew away swiftly, and the Moon arrived in good time for the Council. But the Bat is a lazy good-for-nothing tramp, and he dawdled on the road and played at every turning, and the time passed, and all the guests were assembled, and yet the Sun did not come.

Then the King sent the Dove to call the Sun, and he came very quickly, but the Council had already begun. The Sun explained that the first message had never reached him, and when the King sent to find the Bat, he was brought in tied up like a prisoner. The Sun was very angry and said: "If ever I see you again I will kill you."

Then the King gave the Moon a beautiful cloak of silver and said: "Go and shine on the Earth where Nambi is, so that if she wants to walk at night, she may have your light; and all Nambi's children will love you and rejoice when they see you, and beat drums and make music, and all people on the Earth shall praise you and sing songs to you."

And to the Sun the King said: "I give you a cloak of gold. Wrap it round you all day so that Nambi and her children may not be scorched by your rays. Shine every day on the Earth, and make the trees and gardens and flowers grow, and make the children healthy and strong!"

When the Council was over and all the guests had received their presents, the Sun went out to find the Bat, but he had run away and hidden himself, and no one could find him. To this day the bats hide all through the day under the roofs of houses and in dark corners, and when they see the Sun sinking behind the horizon they peep out, but they know it is not safe to come out of their hiding-places before the Sun has disappeared. And they tell their children and their grandchildren, and in the early dawn, when the first streaks of light appear in the East, all the bats hurry home to their dark corners and stay there snug and safe all day.

But if any foolish young bat stays out too long and the Sun sees him he kills him; for he remembers how the Bat made him late for the King's Council when he might have lost his beautiful present of a golden mantle.

THE STORY OF KASANKE THE LITTLE RED BIRD

ONCE upon a time a lioness and a cow were great friends, and they lived together in a house which they built for themselves.

The lioness had a cub and the cow had a calf, and these two grew up together and played together every day.

The lion cub was a gentle, well-mannered little creature, but the calf was a disobedient, unruly child, and gave great trouble to his mother.

Near the house was a well of fresh water, clear and sweet, and every day the calf played near the well and stirred up the mud, and every day he was punished for doing so. One day the gentle lion cub tried to stop him, and this made him so angry that he pushed the cub into the well and he was drowned. When the calf saw what he had done he was frightened, and ran to find his mother and tell her about it.

The cow was very frightened, too, and she said: "We must both run away, for the lioness will kill us." So they ran to an antelope who lived near by, and the antelope said:

"I will protect you. Am I afraid of a lioness? If she comes here I will drive her away with my horns."

When the lioness got home she found the house empty and no one in the garden, so, as she was very tired, she went to the well to drink, and there she found the body of her cub.

Then she understood that the cow and the calf had run away because they were afraid, and she was very angry and determined to find them and kill them.

First she went to the antelope's house roaring all the way, and when the antelope heard her she forgot her horns and said to the cow: "Run away; if the lioness finds you here she will kill us all."

The King of the Snakes

So the cow and her calf ran on, and they came to the buffalo's house. "I will defend you," said the buffalo. "If the lioness comes here I will trample her with my hoofs."

The lioness came along the road roaring with rage, and when the buffalo heard her he forgot his hoofs and said to the cow: "Run away quickly; if the lioness finds you here she will kill us all."

Then the cow and her calf ran on and came to the elephant's house, and the elephant said: "I will protect you. Am I afraid of a lioness? I will wind my trunk round her and throw her up in the air, and all her bones will break."

But when he heard the lioness coming nearer and nearer, he swayed from side to side, first on one foot and then on the other, and he got so frightened that his trunk rolled up in a big curl, and he said to the cow: "Run away; if the lioness finds you here she will kill us."

The poor cow was exhausted, and she ran a little way and then fell down by the roadside.

Just then Kasanke the Little Red Bird came by and pitied the poor tired cow, and the cow told her the story.

They could hear the lioness roaring in the distance, every moment coming nearer and nearer, but Kasanke was not afraid; she told the cow to hide in the bushes near the road, and she flew quickly to a banana garden and picked a large seed-pod which was dark red and shaped like a heart. Then she brought a bowl and milked the cow, and into the milk she squeezed some red juice till it looked like a bowl of blood.

By this time the lioness was very near, and Kasanke flew to meet her.

"Why are you making such a noise?" she asked.

"Cheeky bird," said the lioness, "I will eat you!"

Kasanke pounced down on the head of the lioness and pecked her eye. The lioness roared with pain and beat the air with her paws, and Kasanke pecked the other eye, and then she threw the bowl of milk over the lioness and the seed-pod at her feet and said:

"Look, I have killed you; your heart has fallen out and you will bleed to death!"

The lioness could not see very well, for her eyes hurt so much, but she was very frightened and ran away and did not stop till she reached her home.

Then the cow thanked Kasanke the Little Red Bird and said: "For ever and ever the cows will love you, and you may come in and out of the kraals as you like. Every kraal shall be your home." And now, all through the country of Uganda, when the cows come into the kraal in the evening to be milked, Kasanke the Little Red Bird follows them, and the cowherds always pour a little milk on the ground before they fill the pails, and the cows turn their heads to see them do it, and are glad, for they know that the milk is for Kasanke the Little Red Bird, who had more courage than all the big animals when the lioness wanted to kill the cow many long years ago.

THE FROG AND THE LIZARD

YOU know that frogs have no tails, and if you look at a lizard's head you will see that its cheeks are puffed out all round its neck; but it was not always so. In Uganda frogs used to have tails, and lizards had quite thin cheeks.

Now I will tell you what happened to alter this:

Once upon a time there was a lizard, who lived on the branches of a cedar-tree, and he made friends with a frog, who lived on a little island in the middle of a pond.

One day the lizard made a feast and called his friend the frog to come to it, but when the frog arrived at the foot of the cedar-tree there was no way for him to climb up, for frogs have feet that are made for swimming, not for climbing trees.

The lizard came running down the tree and said:

"Never mind, I will help you up, I will tie a rope to your tail and pull you after me while I climb."

So he tied a rope to the frog's tail and began to climb, but he pulled so hard that the tail came off and down fell the poor frog to the ground.

He was very angry with the lizard and swam back to his island on the pond thinking all the time how he could revenge himself, and away up in the cedar-tree the lizard was holding his sides with laughter as he told the other guests at his feast how funny the frog looked without a tail.

Some time after this the frog asked the lizard to a feast, and the lizard, thinking that he had forgotten and forgiven the quarrel, said he would like to come.

When he arrived at the pond he wondered how he should get to the island, for he did not know how to swim.

"Never mind," said the frog. "I will tie a rope round your neck and pull you over while I swim." So they started off, but the water was very cold, and when the lizard felt it getting deeper and deeper he got frightened and pulled back.

"Come on," cried the frog, and pulled harder and harder. At last the rope broke and the lizard struggled back to land. He was very nearly drowned and panting for breath, and the rope was so tight round his neck that his cheeks were puffed out all round it. He looked back at the island, and there was the frog laughing at him.

And since that time frogs have had no tails and lizards have puffed-out cheeks. You can see them any day in Uganda, and they are not friends any more.

THE SONG OF THE FOREST WANDERER
(NDABA KUKI BASEBO, BASEBO NDABA KUKI)

OUT of the Forest I wandered
  To lands that were far away,
Seeking the riches of nations,
  No man disputing my sway.
But my heart was heavy with longing,
  Weary my soul with the fray.
What did I think of, my Brothers?
  I thought of the Forest all day.

The Moon that shines on my Forest
  Caressed me with hopes at night.
The Stars that I loved in my childhood
  Soothed me with promises bright.
And the night wind sang in the shadows
  A lullaby soft and light.
What did I dream of, my Brothers?
  I dreamt of the Forest all night.

THE STORY OF THE CHIEF KASUJU

ONCE upon a time a man called Lunzilunzi went into the forest to cut firewood, and he came back with a log and stood it up against a banana-tree, which was a silly thing to do, for a banana-tree is a weak thing, and the log was very heavy.

A child was sitting in the garden, and near by was a sheep, tethered to a stake in the ground, but Lunzilunzi noticed none of these things; he was very tired, and he went into his house to sleep.

Just then some hunters with their dogs came out of the jungle. The dogs frightened the sheep and it jumped away, the rope snapped and the sheep fell against the log, and the log fell on the child and killed it. There was a great noise, everyone talking at once and giving his version of what had happened, and Lunzilunzi came out of his house very angry indeed.

Then the neighbours came up, and there was a great discussion as to who was to blame for the child's death. Some said it was Lunzilunzi's fault, and some said the owner of the sheep was to blame, and some said the hunters with their dogs frightened the sheep and made it fall against the log, which killed the child.

They could not come to any conclusion, so they decided to go to Mengo and let the King's Council settle the case and punish the man who was to blame. So they all set out for Mengo, where the King lives, and on the way they rested in a garden during the heat of the day, and there they found a little boy eating cooked marrows, which are called "ensuju," and the boy asked where they were going, and why they were all so excited. They told him the whole story, and how they were going to the King's Council to have it settled, and the boy said: "I know what I should do if I were the judge; I should settle it very quickly."

They all laughed at the little boy, and they went on their journey, leaving him in the garden eating his "ensuju."

When they arrived at the King's Council and all the chiefs were assembled, they told the story again, but no one could decide who was to blame.

First they said: "Lunzilunzi is to blame." But he said: "My lords, if no one had touched the log it would not have killed the child."

So they said: "The sheep is to blame." But the owner of the sheep said: "My lords, if the dogs had not frightened the sheep it would not have butted the log, which fell on the child and killed it."

So they said: "The dogs are to blame." But the hunter said: "My lords, if the log had not been there the sheep would not have butted it and the child would not have been killed."

So they were back at the beginning again.

Then Lunzilunzi said: "On our way here we rested in a garden, and there we found a little boy eating 'ensuju,' and he said he knew how to decide this case."

So the King sent messengers, and they brought the little boy into the Council Hall.

Then the Katikiro asked him who he was and where he came from, and they told him why the King had sent for him.

The little boy knelt down and held up his left hand and counted his points on the fingers of it with his right hand, beginning with the little finger, and said:

"The law says, a life for a life. The log has killed the child, therefore burn the log.

"The sheep has caused the burning of the log, therefore kill the sheep; and the dogs caused the death of the sheep, therefore kill the dogs.

"The case is finished."

The chiefs were very pleased with the wisdom of the little boy, and the King made him a chief and gave him the title of Kasuju, which means "a little marrow," and said he should decide all the cases between the King's children, and his children should have the chieftainship after him for ever.

And now, in Uganda, if there is any quarrel between the princes or princesses it is not taken to the King's Council to be settled, but the Chief Kasuju hears the case, and his word is law.

THE STORY OF KIBATE

ONCE upon a time there was a man called Kibate who had a great many friends.

Now Kibate wanted to build a house, and he asked his friends about it, and everyone gave him different advice, till at last Kibate thought: "If I take the advice of all my friends my house will be a very queer one, and if I take the advice of one or two the others will be jealous. I had better build my house all alone."

So he went away into the jungle and made a clearing, and lived there alone until his house was finished; and as it took a long time to build Kibate learnt many things, and he made friends with the beasts and birds and trees, and learnt their language.

When his house was finished he made a great feast and called all his friends, and they came gladly, for they had wondered where he was all that time, and some said he was lost.

Everyone praised the house except one man, and he said:

"Kibate, you need one more pole in the roof; if you do not put in one more pole your house will fall down." And he showed him where the pole should go, and Kibate saw that he was right and said:

"I will go into the forest at once and cut a pole. Will you stay here until I come back and help me put it up?" And his friend promised: "I will sit here until you come back."

Then Kibate took his spear and an axe and went into the forest, and he was just going to cut a branch when the tree cried out:

"Kibate, would you hurt an old friend?" So he went to another tree, and it cried out:

"Do not hurt me, Kibate; are we not friends?" And every tree said the same thing, and Kibate went on and on through the forest, but could not find a tree that was not his friend.

At last he was quite tired out, and then he found he had lost his way, and he sat down to think what he should do next.

Just then he heard a rustling in the forest, and a great snake with seven heads came out of the bushes.

Kibate had never seen such a wonderful thing before, and he was more surprised still when each head spoke to him:

"Kibate, the King will send for you."

"Kibate, you shall be a great chief."

"Kibate, you shall be a great warrior."

"Kibate, all Uganda shall hear of you."

"Kibate, the generations to come will praise you."

"Kibate, you shall make fire for the army."

"Kibate, you shall make a rhinoceros laugh."

Then the snake went back again into the bushes, and Kibate got up feeling quite rested, and wondered whether he had really seen the snake or whether he had been asleep and dreamt it.

Very soon he found a way out of the forest and came to a road where many people were passing to and fro.

He asked one man: "Where are all these people going?" And the man told him:

"The King of Uganda is going to war with the King of Ankole, and every man who stays at home will be punished." So Kibate joined the soldiers and went to the war with his spear and his axe.

They marched for many days until they reached the country of Ankole, and then they built a big camp of huts in a wide plain. The next day a dreadful storm fell upon them, and it rained for three nights and three days without stopping, and the camp was soaked and all their things were soaked, and when the rain stopped and the tired soldiers hoped to cook some food there was no fire in the whole camp, so they ate a little raw food and tried to sleep.

But in the night the chief saw a fire on a distant hill, and he woke his men and told them to go there and bring back a pot full of fire with them. So a company of men set out, and when they came to the hill-top they found that the fire was on the horn of a rhinoceros. They begged the rhinoceros to give them some fire, but it said: "It is very dull living alone on the hill-top; the man who can tell me a funny story shall take the fire from my horn."

The men thought and thought, but none of them could think of a funny story, so they had to go back to the camp without the fire. The chief was much troubled, and he sent a proclamation through the army that the man who could tell a funny story to the rhinoceros should be given a chieftainship when the war was over.

When Kibate heard this he volunteered to go all alone and fetch the fire. He reached the distant hill and found the rhinoceros looking out gloomily over the plain, very bored and cross, so he began to tell a story at once:

"Once upon a time there was a King who had no feet."

When the rhinoceros heard this he began to laugh.

"What did the King do?" he asked.

"He walked on his hands," said Kibate.

The rhinoceros laughed and laughed until his sides ached, and Kibate took the fire and kindled the wood in his pot until he had quite a nice blaze, and then he went down to the plain. When he looked back he saw the rhinoceros still laughing on the hill-top! Perhaps you don't think that was a funny story, but, you see, Kibate had lived so long in the jungle that he knew just the sort of story a rhinoceros would find amusing.

KIBATE

TELLS THE RHINOCEROS

A FUNNY STORY

AND:—

MAKES HIM LAUGH!

Kibate returned to the camp and the soldiers made their fires and cooked their food, and the next day they fought a great battle and defeated the army of the King of Ankole.

When the war was over the King sent for Kibate and gave him a chieftainship, and all the soldiers went to their homes and told their relations how Kibate had saved the army, and Kibate went home to his house in the jungle clearing to get his things, and there he found his friend sitting just where he had left him, but he had grown very old, for he had sat there thinking all the time, and thinking always makes people get very old.

THE STORY OF THE GOLDEN-CRESTED CRANE

ONCE upon a time there was a King of Uganda who had a little daughter called Namirembe, which means "Peace." She was a sweet child, and everybody loved her, and as she grew up she was kind to all her father's subjects, and loved all the animals and birds and flowers in her father's kingdom.

Every year the King went to the Sesse Islands to visit Mukasa the old wizard, and sometimes he took Peace with him.

The chief Gabunga prepared the two big war canoes, which were called "Waswa" and "Mbaliga," and a fleet of smaller ones and hundreds of paddlers to take the King over the blue waters to the Sesse Islands.

Peace loved the big war canoes with their high red prows ornamented with antelope horns and parrots' feathers and shells and beads and strips of leather. At the stern of one of the canoes the chief had a grass shelter built, and Peace and her nurse sat under this when the sun was hot.

The islanders have many songs, and they sing all the time they are paddling; sometimes one man sings and they all join in the chorus, and they keep time with their paddles.

They sang this "Song of Princess Peace":

> What shall our song to the Princess be?–
>   Over the waters to Sesse.
> Tell her the wonderful things she will see
>   In our beautiful islands of Sesse.
>   Smooth, yellow sands,
>   High, rocky fells,
>   Deep, dark forests,
>   Cool, green dells.
> And the wizard Mukasa is weaving his spells

Away on the islands of Sesse.
  Paddles to left,
  Paddles to right;
 Swing them all up in the air
How we shall sing on the islands to-night,
  Because our Princess will be there.

One day Peace asked her father: "Why do we always go to the same islands when there are so many in the Great Lake?" And the King told her:

"All the islands in the Great Lake do not belong to my kingdom; if we went there the people would kill us; they are another nation, and they have another language."

But Peace said: "I should like to go and see people who are different from us, and see their customs, and hear their strange language." And her father laughed and said:

"Little Princess, do not travel in far countries; there is much for you to learn in your own beautiful land."

Still Peace always thought of the other islands and the strange countries that lie beyond the blue waters of the Great Lake.

One morning very early Peace was picking up loquats under a tree in her father's garden when a big crane came by, leaning forward as he walked and lifting his feet very high in the queer way all cranes have. He greeted the little Princess and told her he was going that day to Kavirondo to see his brother who had fever

"Where is Kavirondo?" asked Peace.

"Far away over the Great Lake," answered the crane. "It is a wild country, and the people have strange customs, and a language which is hard to understand."

"Oh, if only I could go with you!" said Peace.

"Why not?" said the crane. "If you are not afraid you can sit on my back and hold on to my feathers. My wings will keep you from falling off, and if you get giddy you can shut your eyes; but you must be brave and hold on very tightly, for it is a long journey, and we cannot stop in the middle. If you let go you will fall into the Great Lake and be drowned. We shall return this evening."

Peace climbed on the crane's back, and he stretched his long neck, and put out his long legs behind him, and they started on their journey. Right over the blue waters they flew, passing the little islands, some of them so small that no one lives on them, only the diver birds who eat fish make their nests on the rocks.

Once they passed a flock of grey parrots with red tails, and called to them:

"Where are you going?"

"We are going to Kyagwe," they called back, "for we hear that the loquats and wild plums are ripe."

Then they left the islands far behind, and there was nothing round them but sky and water and golden sunshine.

Peace thought it all very beautiful, and she never forgot to hold very tightly to the crane's feathers and to sit quietly right in the middle of his broad back.

At last they saw the shores of Kavirondo in the distance, and when they were well over the land the crane flew downwards.

They stopped near a great rock, and Peace got down and looked round her, wondering at all she saw. Great dark hills jutting out into the Lake, the plain stretching for miles and miles round her, and beyond it the rugged Nandi escarpment, all so strange and different from the green slopes of Uganda.

The crane showed her a little crevice in the rock where it was cool and shady, and where she could sit comfortably and look down on the path below and see the people passing, and perhaps hear their language. Then the crane flew away to see his sick brother. Peace saw some Kavirondo warriors coming down the path; they wore helmets made of cowrie shells and big bunches of ostrich feathers, and they wore no clothes but beads, and had painted themselves white and yellow and red; and then some women passed, and Peace was rather shocked because they wore no clothes–only beads and shells and tags of leathers. She looked away over the plain and saw their villages, several houses together with a big fence round, and fields of grain outside, no green banana gardens or fruit-trees or grass.

Then the crane came back and said it was time to return or they would not reach Uganda before dark; so they started on again over the blue water towards the setting Sun, and when Peace saw the islands and the green shores in the distance she laughed for joy and said:

"My beautiful country of Uganda, I shall never want to leave it again."

The big islands looked pink below them, and the crane explained that the millet harvest was ripe and the fields looked rose-coloured in the setting Sun.

Then they reached the King's palace, and Peace ran to her father and told him where she had been and all she had seen that wonderful day, and the King called the crane and thanked him for taking care of the little Princess and said:

"I will give you a present of a golden crest with a little black bit at the foot of it, and you shall always wear it in memory of this day."

The crane was very pleased, and lifted his feet higher than ever when he walked, and all the little cranes who were born after that had golden crests on their heads, and from that time they have been called "Golden-Crested Cranes."

And if you go to Kavirondo you will still see the path by which Peace sat, only now it is a broad road and goes from Kisumu to Mumias, and perhaps you can find the rock on which she sat in the comfortable little crevice the crane found for her.

THE SONG OF THE GREY HERON
(SEKANYOLYA)

MARSH flowers are my curtain,
  Soft rushes my bed,
The green feathered papyrus
  Waves over my head.

Dark grey are the shadows,
  Dark brown is the pool,
The soft moonlight above me
  Shines silver and cool.

The night wind croons while I slumber,
  The ripples rock me to sleep,
The most beautiful place in this beautiful world
  Is my home in the marshes deep.

THE STORY OF THE GREY HERON

IN a lovely swamp on the borders of a river lived a family of grey herons. Each one was tall and thin, with a long graceful neck and a thin pointed beak, and they were a very grave family. None of them ever smiled; they stood in the water for hours together quite silently, and every now and then they ate up something that passed by.

One day the old father heron was standing near the swamp-bridge, nearly hidden by the shady papyrus which waved far over his head, when a frog hopped on to the bridge. At that moment a snake wriggled out of the grass, and stopped in front of the frog. The frog was terrified, but he pretended to be brave.

"Where are you going?" said the snake.

"I have been to the Capital to see my cousins," answered the frog; "and I am returning to my home on the other side of the swamp."

"What is the news in the Capital?" asked the snake.

"They have made a new law," said the frog; "he who assaults his neighbour on the high road will be killed."

"Really," said the snake, laughing; "and who will kill him?"

"The King's soldiers, who are dressed in grey barkcloth," said the frog.

"Well, let them come," laughed the snake, and he opened his mouth to eat the frog; but at that moment the grey heron, who had been standing silently listening to the conversation, suddenly darted forward and picked up the snake in his beak, and held him wriggling in the air.

"Didn't I tell you," said the frog, "that he who assaults his neighbour on the high road will be killed?"

Then the grey heron gobbled up the snake. The frog thanked him very much for saving his life, and he stayed a little while, telling him the news of the Capital.

Just then an eagle flew over the swamp carrying a large branch in his talons. Something must have startled him, for he dropped the branch; the frog saw it dropping and hopped out of the way, but he did not warn the grey heron, and the branch fell on the poor bird and broke his neck.

The other herons came hurrying up and were very angry with the frog.

"Our father saved your life, you ungrateful creature," they said, "and now you let him be killed; if ever we meet you or your children again we will kill you."

Then they took the old grey heron away and made him a beautiful grave under the papyrus where the pink and blue water-lilies grow. And ever since that time grey herons always eat frogs.

I don't think they could ever have been great friends, even in the old days, for the grey herons are quiet, dignified birds, and the frogs have always been noisy chatterboxes, who talk all night when nice people are in bed and asleep.

THE CRIMSON-STRIPED LILY

THERE was once a very beautiful little Prince born in Uganda. One day when his nurse had put him to sleep under a cedar-tree in the garden a great eagle swooped down and carried him away to her nest on the distant purple hills.

The eagle had meant to eat him, but when she saw what a beautiful child he was she pitied him, and kept him to play with her little eaglets in the nest, and the eagles became his friends, and he learnt their language and many wonderful things about the birds and beasts and flowers.

One day the eagle brought two kids to the nest, and the Prince begged her not to eat them, so the eagle gave him the kids, and they grew up in the nest too.

When they were quite big goats the little Prince took them to the hill-side every day, and they played there with the other animals.

When the spring rains came the forests and jungles and swamps and hills were covered with flowers. Great white lilies, five on a stalk, and tiger-lilies of yellow and red, and ground-orchids purple and yellow and white, and some so queer that they looked like bumble-bees, and little rock-flowers, and water-lilies pink and blue and mauve, and many other beautiful things; the little Prince knew them all by name.

One day he was out on the hill-side and he trod on a sharp stone and cut his foot very deeply. The blood poured out, and he could not tie it up to stop the bleeding. All his friends hurried up and tried to help, but none of them could stop the bleeding.

Then the tall lily took her pure white petals and laid them on the wound and the bleeding stopped, but the petals were stained with blood, a broad crimson streak.

Then they called the eagle and told her what had happened. "Little Prince," she said, "you have been with us long enough; it is time you returned to your own people, for what should we do if harm came to the son of the King?"

So the Prince said good-bye to his friends, and the eagle carried him away to Mengo, where the King lived. The King and his chiefs were in the Council when a messenger came to say that a great eagle was circling round the house with a child in her talons. They all went out to see, and the eagle laid the little Prince at his father's feet, and the people called him "Prince Eagle "from that day.

There was great rejoicing, and the King sat up all night listening to the stories about the jungle which the Prince told him.

Then the King said: "It was the lily that saved my child's life; let me go and thank her myself." So they went to the distant purple hills and found the lily, and the King said:

"I have heard what you did, and I have come to thank you. For ever and ever you shall wear a broad crimson stripe on every petal, that all the people may remember that you saved the life of the King's son."

THE COOKING-POT AND THE DRUM

ONCE upon a time two brothers lived in one village; one was a potter and the other was a drum-maker.

One day the potter found some beautiful clay, and he brought it home and prepared it carefully until it was as fine as powder, and he mixed the clay very smoothly with water, and made it into a cooking-pot, large and smooth and round, and he made an ornamental border round the edge, and put fresh grass down in his courtyard and left the pot to dry in the sun.

When the cooking-pot was dry he baked it in a kiln, very carefully seeing that the fire was not too hot, and when he took it out of the kiln it was the most beautiful cooking-pot he had ever made. Meanwhile his brother, the drum-maker, had been at work. He found a log of good wood, and hollowed it out and shaped it with an adze, and smoothed the wood with rough sandpaper leaves.

Then he bought a beautiful cow-skin and stretched a piece over the top, and another piece over the bottom, and joined the pieces together with long strips of twisted hide, and when it was finished it was the most beautiful drum he had ever made.

The two brothers rejoiced very much over their work, and their friends rejoiced, too, and said:

"These things are fit for a King." And the cooking-pot and the drum heard what was said, and because they were foolish creatures they were very much flattered, as though the credit of being beautiful was all their own, and they became so vain and silly that at last they quarrelled as to which was the most beautiful, and none of their friends could decide between them.

Now a very mischievous monkey was passing by and heard them quarrelling, and inquired the cause.

So they told him, and he said:

"If I decide this case will you abide by my judgment?" And they both promised:

"What you say shall be law."

So the monkey said: "Make a fire and put the drum on it, and beat the cooking-pot with drumsticks, and then you will see which is the most beautiful." And when they did this the cooking-pot broke in pieces and the drum shrivelled up and was burnt.

When the monkey saw what was done he danced for joy and shouted, but the two brothers returned while he was still doing this, and they were very angry and speared him, for they saw that it was his mischievous advice which had spoilt all their beautiful work.

This story has a moral, but you must find that out for yourself.

THE STORY OF THE FAIRY FOXES

A LONG time ago there was a King of Uganda who wanted to make a Zoo, and he called all his chiefs together and told them to bring animals of every kind from the forests and jungles and swamps

Then he planted a beautiful garden and put cages into it, and people came from all over the country to see it. But the animals were very miserable; night and day they thought of their homes, and they hated having food brought to them instead of hunting for it themselves, and they hated having water brought to them in water-pots instead of drinking it from the deep forest pools, but no one was sorry for them except the King's dwarf, and he had lived in the jungle and knew their language.

One day when the King was walking in his Zoo and the dwarf was with him, he said:

"Am I not a great King? No one has ever made a Zoo like this before, in which all the animals of the country are collected together." But the dwarf said:

"All the animals are not here; there is one animal which lives in the Mukono Forest which no chief has brought, because, though it cries all night and everyone hears it, no man has ever seen it. Some people say it is a bat, and some say it is a sloth, and some say it is a fairy fox with wings made of the night mists."

When the King heard this he said:

"I will not be beaten by any animal; I will go to Mukono and fetch this fairy animal myself." So he sent for Sekibobo the chief and told him to build a big encampment near the forest, and the men worked night and day till it was finished. Then the King and his whole court went to Mukono.

For three months the King lived in the encampment, and every night he went into the forest, but though he heard the fairy foxes crying all round him he never saw one. Sometimes the sound came from above his head, but there was nothing there; and sometimes it came from the ground at his feet, but there was nothing there; and sometimes to the right hand and sometimes to the left, but nothing was there; and the people called them "enjoga," which means "bullies," because they teased the King every night.

At last the time came to return to the capital, and the King sat sadly in his house, and the dwarf sat near him and said:

"Why is the King so sad?" And the King answered:

"I am sorry I have no fairy fox for my Zoo, but there is another reason. I have learnt to love the beautiful forests and jungles and the deep glades and shady paths and water pools, and the moonlight nights are never so lovely in the capital as they are in the country, and I am sad that I must leave it all and return."

Then the dwarf said: "If you are so sad at leaving the country after only three months, how much more sad must the animals be, for this is their home, and in your wonderful Zoo they are only prisoners."

When the King heard that he was thoughtful and silent for some time, and then he called Sekibobo and said: "Send a messenger quickly to the capital and tell the Katikiro that all the animals in the Zoo are to be sent home, everyone to his own forest or jungle or swamp." "I will have no more prisoners," he said.

And now there is a broad road which goes from Kampala to Jinja and passes quite near to the Mukono Forest, and if you go there you will hear the "enjoga "crying in the forest all night, but no one has ever seen them. Some people say they are bats, and some say they are sloths, and some say they are fairy foxes with wings made of the night mists.

THE LOCUSTS

STANDING all alone in the middle of a great plain is Mount Elgon. Long ago Mount Elgon was a volcano, and there is a crater on the top which is eight miles across.

Once upon a time a mischievous young wizard lived on Mount Elgon, and he stirred up the fire in the crater until the flames blazed up to the sky, and when the people who lived in the plains below were frightened and ran away the wizard threw great rocks after them; some of the rocks were as big as houses. You can see them lying about on the plains to this day. But as the wizard grew older he grew kinder, and left off throwing stones and let the fire die down in the crater till there was just a little left which puffed like a steam engine sometimes, but did no harm; and the people returned to the mountain and climbed up its beautiful green slopes and built houses and planted gardens and were quite happy, and the wizard sat on the top and was happy too.

One day the people in Uganda heard a queer sound like a storm in the distance, and a great black cloud was moving swiftly along, but it did not seem like the usual storms.

They ran out of their houses to look, and the old men said: "This is no storm; it is a flight of locusts."

Then the locusts settled down on the land and ate up everything. From province to province they went till there was nothing green left in the country.

When the wizard on Mount Elgon looked out over the land and saw how the locusts had spoiled it he was very angry, and he sent a hornet with a message to the wizard of the Sesse Islands telling him about it and said:

"If you will persuade the locusts to fly over the Great Lake I will raise a hurricane and blow them into the water."

The King of the Snakes

When the wizard of the Sesse Islands heard about the locusts he was very angry, too, and he sent the hornet back with a message telling the wizard to get his hurricane ready for the next morning.

Then he called all the fireflies together and said: "Go over to the mainland and sing to the locusts all night while they are resting on the ground and persuade them to cross the Lake."

So the fireflies flew over at sunset, and all night they sang this song as they danced in and out of the shadows:

> Over the water of sparkling blue,
>   Dancing in golden light,
> Lie beautiful islands of every hue,
>   The Country of Heart's Delight.
>
> Deep, cool forests and crystal streams,
>   Fruit trees and fields of gold,
> These are the islands of boyhood's dreams,
>   Where no one ever grows old.

The locusts have no King to teach them wisdom, and they did not know how big the Lake was (for you could put Scotland into it), and they thought because they saw islands near the shore there would be more beautiful ones lying far out, so when they heard the fireflies' song they decided to go to the Country of Heart's Delight, and in the morning they rose up from the ground in bands and began to fly over the Lake.

Then the wizard from Mount Elgon hurled his hurricane upon them, and they were swept into the water and drowned, and millions and millions and millions of dead locusts were floating on the waters for days afterwards.

That is why the old people in Uganda still call the Lake the Locust-Killer, but the children learn to call it Lake Victoria, for that is its name on the map.

THE STORY OF THE HIPPOS

ONCE upon a time there was a King of Uganda who loved the animals very much and made a law to protect them, and no man was allowed to kill an animal in the forests or jungles or swamps, and he sent a messenger to the Big Grey Elephant to tell him this.

There was great rejoicing among the animals, for they never want to kill men, only they don't like being hunted.

For many years there was peace in the land, and men walked by night without spears and were quite safe.

One day the King wished to send an order to the chiefs of Busoga, and the messenger walked all through Kyagwe until he came to the Nile. That day there had been a terrific storm on the Lake: great waves thundered against the shore, and the waters rushed over the Ripon Falls into the river like a flood, and the canoes by which people cross into Busoga were washed away, and even the huts of the canoe men on the bank were carried away by the water, and when the King's messenger arrived on the bank there was no way for him to get across.

He sat down sadly and wondered what he should do (for a King's messenger cannot return until he has fulfilled his mission), when an old hippo came up and asked him what was the matter.

The man said: "I am the King's messenger, and I am taking an order to the chiefs of Busoga, but the storm has swept away the canoes and I cannot cross."

Then the hippo said: "Wait until the storm is over and we will help you across."

And he went away and called all the other hippos together, and they came where the King's messenger sat. And when the storm was over and the sun shone brightly again the hippos went down into the water, and they made a floating bridge with their bodies and the King's messenger went over safely.

And now if you go to the Ripon Falls you will see a notice:

VISITORS ARE REQUESTED
NOT TO SHOOT
THE HIPPOS.

And on moonlight nights when the Great Lake stretches like a sheet of silver away to the horizon, and the water dashes over the Falls sending showers of silver sparks against the rocks, the hippos climb slowly up the bank and read this notice and rejoice, for they remember the days of the good King who protected the animals, and they think he has come back to rule over the land.

THE LEOPARD AND THE GOAT AND THEIR FRIENDS

ONCE upon a time a leopard and a goat were great friends, and they lived together, and the leopard had two little cubs and the goat had two little kids, and the children played together and were very happy. But every day the kids grew fatter and fatter, and every day the cubs grew thinner and thinner, and the leopard became very jealous and began to hate the goat.

At last she thought of a wicked plan; she said to the goat: "My cousins who live across the valley are making a big feast this afternoon and I have promised them a surprise; will you go to the barkcloth makers and buy me a very beautiful cloth to wear at the feast?"

While the goat was away the leopard caught the two little kids and tied their mouths to keep them from crying out, and made them into a parcel packed in wide banana-leaves tied up with fibre, and he brought the parcel and put it down in the courtyard.

Now the wild cat and the guinea-fowl were great friends and they often visited the leopard and the goat, and it so happened that they were passing through the garden and saw what the leopard did, but they hid behind a tree and said nothing.

When the leopard returned to the house they followed her as if they had only just arrived, and the leopard greeted them and told them about the feast.

Just then the goat returned, and the leopard took the barkcloth and went to dress.

Then the wild cat and the guinea-fowl told the goat what they had seen in the garden, and they all three went quickly to the parcel and released the poor little kids, and they caught the leopard cubs and tied *them* up, and put *them* into a parcel, and put the parcel back where it was before in the courtyard.

When the leopard was dressed in the new barkcloth she came in feeling very grand, and said to the goat:

"Will you carry that parcel for me? It is my contribution to the feast, and a *great* surprise for my cousins." So the goat took up the parcel, and the wild cat and the guinea-fowl said:

"We will go with you across the valley."

As they went they asked each other riddles.

The goat asked: "What is it that goes the same journey every day?" And the wild cat guessed: "The sun."

Then she asked: "What is it that has no feet and yet travels all over the country?" And the guinea-fowl guessed: "Dried fish."

Then she asked a riddle: "In what land are there no women, only men?" This they discussed for some time, and the guinea-fowl told them: "A patch of Indian corn," for all the corn cobs have long beards, like old men. The wild cat didn't think this a very good riddle; but the goat did.

The leopard guessed nothing, and being rather cross, she said:

"You all think you are very clever to-day." And the goat said:

"We are cleverer to-day than we have ever been before, but we shall have to be cleverer still before the sun goes down."

When they reached the village across the valley the leopard said to his cousins:

"I have brought you a most beautiful stew; it must be cooked just as it is, tied up in banana-leaves. Do not open it until it is cooked, and you will be very surprised when you see the contents."

So they put the parcel into a big cooking-pot, and the three friends ran very quickly home, and the wild cat and the guinea-fowl helped the goat pack up all her things, and they took the two little kids and fled to the forest and made a new home there, for they knew now that the leopard hated them and would kill them all when she found out the trick they had played her.

Meanwhile at the leopard's feast the guests were getting hungry, and at last the stew was cooked, and they all sat down and undid the parcel, wondering what the great surprise would be, and what did they see but two poor little cooked leopard cubs.

They were very angry with the leopard and said: "You heartless creature to cook your own children." The leopard cried:

"I did not cook them, the goat has played me a trick; let us go and kill her and her kids."

So all the leopards went across the valley with their cousin, but the goat and her kids had gone away long before they reached the house, and they never caught them, and since that day leopards and goats have hated each other.

Afterwards the wild cat and the guinea-fowl had a quarrel, and became enemies, but that is rather a spiteful story, so I won't tell it to you; they said dreadful things to each other which are best forgotten.

THE STRANGER

ONCE upon a time the King of Uganda went to Koja to see his herd of cows, and while he was there a strange thing happened.

The people near Mount Elgon saw a white patch high up on the mountain, and they said: "It is snow." But the patch moved down the mountain side, and they said: "It is a cloud." But still it moved on, and when it reached the foot-hills they saw that it was a flight of snow-white birds.

No one had ever seen such birds before; they flew on over the plain towards the Lake, right across the Great Lion River, which is really a country all to itself.

People lived in the river on little islands made of reeds and papyrus, one house on each island and a canoe tied up near the door, and they have no roads; the river is their only road when they go to the banks to buy and sell.

They have their own customs and their own language. The birds did not stop on the river islands; they flew right over into Busoga till they came to the Nile, and then they crossed the Nile and flew right over the forests and hills of Kyagwe till they came to Koja, where the King was, and they settled down on the herd of cows.

All the people marvelled to see these snow-white birds, and the King said: "This is a good omen; something fortunate will happen to the country." Then he went back to the capital and the Katikiro met him and said: "A stranger has arrived in the country; he is different from any man we have ever seen, and he has a little child with him."

The King commanded them to bring the stranger before him, and when he came he asked him questions, but he knew no language that the chiefs knew, only a few words of Swahili, which were no use.

At first the people thought he ought to be killed, for they said: "He is different from any man we have ever seen; perhaps he is a spy sent to prepare the way for some enemy who will eat up our country."

But the King remembered the white birds and said: "I will not kill him; he will bring good fortune to the country."

Then he called an old chief whom he loved and trusted and said: "Take away this man, and take care of him and his child; teach him Luganda and our customs; some day he will bring us good fortune."

So the old chief took the stranger to his home and gave him a house to live in and a garden, and boys to wait on him, and an old woman to take care of the child, for she was a little girl, and every day he taught him Luganda, and they became great friends, and at last he was able to speak, and the chief took him to the King.

Then the King asked him many questions about his country and his people, and what his name was, but when he said it no man could pronounce it, it was too difficult.

And every day the King called him, and the people all knew that the stranger was the King's friend, and they called him "Mugenyi," which means "Stranger," because they could not pronounce his name.

The little girl grew up different from all the other children in Uganda. She had long golden hair and blue eyes, and a skin like milk, and she grew strong and big, and the people loved her and called her "Joy" or "Snowbird"; but her father said: "Her name is Sorrow."

After some time the King heard that a great army was marching against his country, and he collected his soldiers and made his chiefs generals over them, and prepared to march to Budu, where the enemy was advancing.

Then Stranger said: "I will go with you and teach the chiefs how to build a great fort, and we will stop the enemies of the King from crossing the border."

So the King gave him the command of the army, and they marched to Budu and built a great fort and drove back the enemy and killed thousands of warriors, and when those who were left saw Stranger commanding the Baganda they were afraid, for he wore strange clothes made of barkcloth, and they said: "He is a wizard; we cannot fight against him."

So the enemy was utterly beaten, and the Baganda went back to their homes victorious.

Then the King was much pleased and gave Stranger many presents and cows, and the old chief loved him more and more, and they swore the oath of friendship, which is the most sacred oath in the world.

As the years went on the old chief noticed that his friend looked sorrowful and sad, and that he sat alone on the hill-side looking over the Great Lake, with only little Sorrow near him, and that he often looked at the child with eyes that were full of tears, and one day he said to him:

"My brother, I am grieved to see you so changed. Cannot you tell your sorrow to me, your great friend?" And Stranger said:

"Come away with me to the hill-side and I will tell you."

So the two friends and little Sorrow set out at sunset, and when they reached a shady spot on the hill-side overlooking the Great Lake they sat down, and the child chased butterflies and picked flowers round them.

For a long time they were silent, and then Stranger spoke: "I came to you a stranger, full of sorrow, and you made me welcome, and I learnt your language and your customs, and your country became my country, and I never meant to leave Uganda, but now I look at my little child and I know that I was wrong; I must return to my own people, for a girl must be brought up by the women of her father's tribe."

Then he told the old chief who he was and all his history, and the old man listened silently, for though he had often wondered, all these years, he had never asked questions.

Little Sorrow came and sat on her father's knee, and soon she fell asleep, and the moon rose over the lake, and the stars twinkled in the dark sky, and still the two friends sat on the hill-side while Stranger poured out his history.

And the old chief said: "You are right; a girl must be brought up by the women of her father's tribe." The next day they went to the King, and told him Stranger's decision, and the King was very sorrowful and said to the old chief: "Is it well?" And he answered: "It is well."

All the chiefs and people were very sorry when they heard that Stranger was going, and brought them many presents, and Sorrow said good-bye to all her friends, and the old chief saw them safely across the borders of Uganda. And when he returned to the capital he found everyone talking of Stranger and the little girl, and telling each other about them, and wondering who they really were and where their country and home really was; but the old chief alone was silent, for he alone knew the real history of Stranger and the secret of his life, and sometimes in the evening he would climb the hill-side and sit where he had sat with his friend, and the tears would roll down his cheeks, for he knew that he would never see him again.

And if you go to the province of Budu you will see the fort which Stranger helped the King to build, for the ruins are still there, and the snowbirds never left Uganda, you will always see them with the cows; but if you ask about little "Joy," whom her father called Sorrow, the people will shake their heads and say: "Perhaps there was a little girl, perhaps it was a spirit, perhaps it was only a snowbird–who knows?"

Only the old chief ever knew who Stranger really was, and a Muganda will never betray the secret of his friend.

THE LION, THE HYENA, AND THE HARE

OF all the animals in the forest the hare is the wisest, and the animals all know this.

Most of the animals hunt at night and sleep during the day, but the hare sleeps all night in his cosy little house and spends the day wide awake learning things. Sometimes he hides under a bush or the thick grass by the roadside, and his bright little eyes see all that passes, and he knows all about men and their customs, and he has learnt their language, so he understands what they are talking about.

In Uganda there is a great forest called the Mabira Forest, and once upon a time the animals in it were very unhappy, for they were ruled over by an old king lion who was fierce and cruel, and had only one friend in the forest, the hyena, who always went hunting with him and ate up any scraps the king lion left.

The hyena was a good-for-nothing, useless creature, who never did anything for anybody, a stupid animal with no brains and an idiotic laugh which all the other animals found most annoying.

Of all the creatures in the forests the one who hated him most was the hare.

Every night when he had settled down to sleep the lion would come by roaring on his way to hunt, and when he had passed and the hare had cuddled down again to sleep the hyena would pass, laughing in his silly way.

At last the animals could stand it no longer, and the hare thought of a plan to be rid of both of them.

"Sir," he said to the king lion, "I have bought a piece of land and want to farm it, but I am a weak and foolish creature; will you go into partnership with me and protect me?" The lion consented, for he thought in his cruel heart: "If there is any trouble I will eat up the hare and the land will be mine. "

"Let us have the hyena as third partner," said the hare; "he is so wise and so much respected in the forest."

The hyena was very much pleased, for he was too stupid to see that this was only flattery; he just laughed.

"Let us go and see this land at once," said the lion. So they started out.

"It is very dull just walking along," said the hare; "let us play a game as we go."

"What game can we play?" said the lion crossly. "All games are so silly."

"I know a nice game," said the hare. "If anyone trips he must tell the others what he was thinking about, and if it isn't interesting they will eat him."

The two partners agreed, for they knew the little hare couldn't eat *them*.

On they went, and suddenly the hare tripped. "What were you thinking about?" said the lion. "I was thinking," said the hare, "how the rocks grow. Is there as much under the ground as above?"

"That is a great thought," said the lion; "anyone might trip thinking that." So they went on.

Suddenly the hare tripped again. "What were you thinking about?" they asked him. "I was thinking," said the hare, "what happens to all the barkcloths. Every year the cloth-makers take the bark from the tree, and hammer it into barkcloth with mallets, and dry it in the Sun, and every year people buy new barkcloths. There must be thousands and thousands of barkcloths in the country; one would think they would be lying about in heaps, but it is not so."

"That is a great idea," said the lion, "and enough to make anyone trip."

The hyena just laughed, and they went on again. Suddenly the hyena tripped.

"What were you thinking of?" they asked. But the hyena had never thought of anything in his life; he just laughed in his silly way, and the lion said: "We will eat him now, I am hungry." But the hare said: "You may have my share; I don't eat hyenas," and he lay down and rested in the cool grass while the lion ate up his only friend.

When they started off again the hare said: "There is a hill over there from which there is a lovely view right over the River Nile, but I don't think we have time to go there."

"If I say there is time there *is* time," said the lion. "Let us go at once." So they began to climb the hill. At the top there were two great rocks with a narrow path between them, and the hare ran ahead to show the way, and the lion followed, but he was so fat after his big meal that he got stuck halfway through, and the hare rolled down a rock from above to block the path behind him, and the lion could not go either backwards or forwards, and he roared with rage.

Then the hare ran back to the forest and called the other animals to come to kill the lion, but when they arrived they found him dead. Then they all returned rejoicing, and chose the big grey elephant to be their king, and for many years there was peace and happiness in the Mabira Forest.

HOW THE HARE TRADED WITH A BAG OF CORN

THE big grey elephant and the hare were great friends, and they decided to make a wheat farm together on the hare's land.

But when they began the work was too heavy for the little hare, and he said: "You do all the clearing and I will sow the seed."

So the elephant cleared the land with his trunk, and ploughed it with his tusks, and broke up the big lumps of earth with his feet, and when the ground was ready he gave the hare the corn to sow. But the hare's hands were so small he could not manage it, and he said: "You sow the seed, I will do the weeding." So the elephant did the sowing; but when it came to weeding the hare was so slow that the elephant said: "I will do the weeding; you shall do the harvesting." And when the harvest was ripe the hare had fever, so the elephant did all the work and they sold the corn in the market for a good price.

Then the hare said: "How can I take my share when I did none of the work? Give me some corn and I will go and trade with it."

So the elephant gave him a handful of corn, and he put it into his little white bag and went off on the road to the capital to make his fortune. The first person he met was a very hungry guinea-fowl, and directly he showed him the corn he gobbled it up.

Then the hare sat down and pretended to cry: "Oh, what shall I do? That corn was not mine; it belonged to the big grey elephant." Then the guinea-fowl said: "I will give you an egg; go and trade with that, it is more valuable than the corn."

So the hare went on till he came to a place where wild plums grew, and some men had made a heap of stones and were throwing them up at the plums.

The hare put the egg carefully down on the heap of stones and went to pick up plums, when one of the men, without looking, picked up the egg and threw it instead of a stone, and it broke. The hare pretended to cry: "Oh, what shall I do? The egg was not mine; the guinea-fowl gave it to me because he ate the corn which belonged to the big grey elephant. What shall I trade with now?" The men said: "You may keep the plums you have picked up and trade with them."

So the hare went on till he came to a hornbill sitting on the branch of a cedar-tree by the roadside, and making the most awful noise, like three old crows cawing together.

Now once upon a time the hornbill had quite a nice voice, but she was so vain about it, and was always trying to sing such high top notes, that her voice broke, and unfortunately all her children inherited it, and now they are for ever telling the other birds and animals what a beautiful voice their mother once had, and how much it was admired, and all the jungle is tired of hearing about it.

The hare greeted her politely and told her of his adventures, and the hornbill said: "Well, you won't get much for wild plums in this country; give them to me and take in exchange two of my beautiful tail feathers."

She gave him two large black-and-white feathers, and while the hare was tucking them into his bag she began: "Once I had an exquisite voice and was much admired." The little hare didn't wait to hear the old story all over again; he just waved his hand and ran down the road. Before long he came to a river, and as he stooped down to drink the feathers fell out of his bag into the water and were carried away by the current.

The hare wrung his hands on the bank. "Oh, river," he cried, "give me back my feathers!" But the Fairy of the River far below in the deep water called back to him: "A river is like the life of man; it never returns. What is past is done; take some of my pure water and trade with that."

So the hare filled his little water-bottle and went on till he came to a blacksmith's forge, but the blacksmiths were all sitting under a tree and doing no work. "Why do you not work?" asked the hare.

"We have no water for the forge," answered the blacksmiths. "Give us the water in your bottle, and you shall have an axe."

So the hare gave them the water and went on his way, carrying the axe, until he came to a market-place where the butcher had killed a cow, but he could not cut up the meat, for his knife was broken.

"Give me your axe," he cried when he saw the hare, "and I will give you the cow's head."

So the hare gave him the axe and went on down the road dragging the cow's head after him till he came to a marsh on the borders of a big river. On the banks were herds of cattle, and the herdsmen were resting under the palm-trees near the marsh.

The little hare was hot and weary, and tired of dragging the heavy head, so he sat down and thought out a trick to make his fortune. He pulled the cow's head after him over the marsh and fixed it firmly between two tufts of reeds.

Then he ran along the river bank, crying: "Help! Help! Help!" The herdsmen came running up when they heard his cries.

"Look!" cried the hare, "the cow is drowning in the marsh. I am the servant of the big grey elephant, and that is his cow. I was going to trade with it, but now it is drowning. What shall I do?"

The herdsmen were very sorry for him, but they said: "We cannot cross the marsh to pull it out, we shall sink in ourselves, but you can run across with a rope and tie it to the cow's horns and then we will pull it out for you."

So one of them ran for a rope, and the hare crossed the marsh lightly to the cow's head and tied it to the horns, and the herdsmen pulled and suddenly the head came out with a jerk. "See what you have done!" cried the little hare. "You have pulled the head off the big grey elephant's cow." But the herdsmen laughed very much, for they saw the trick he had played on them, and they said: "Oh, little hare, we have often heard of you; stay with us in the kraals to-night and tell us stories of the jungle and forest, and to-morrow we will give you a cow."

So the hare slept that night in the kraals with Kasanke the little red bird whom the cows love, and told the herdsmen many strange tales of life in the Mabira Forest, and the next morning they gave him a beautiful white cow with long horns.

And he went home driving his cow before him, and the big grey elephant was pleased and praised him very much, and they were greater friends than ever.

THE FOOLISH HARE

ONCE upon a time there was a family of six hares, who were all of them wise except one, who was the youngest, and although his brothers tried in every way to teach him and keep him from doing silly things, the other animals in the forest soon found out that at last there had been born a hare who was a fool.

One day this foolish hare was walking alone in the forest when he met a crafty old leopard, who said: "I was just coming to see you; I am in rather a difficulty, and I want you to lend me three goats." The foolish hare was quite flattered that a big animal like a leopard should borrow from him, and he ran home quickly and fetched the goats.

"I will pay you the day after to-morrow," said the leopard. But time passed, and no payment arrived, so the hare went to the leopard's house and said: "If you cannot pay me I shall have to tell my brothers, for I have to give them an account of all my things."

The leopard said: "I was just thinking of that debt when you arrived, and to-morrow I am going to fetch my goats from the islands and I will pay you, but if you have never been to the islands perhaps you would like to come with me."

The hare thought it would be a great adventure, and he foolishly said in his heart: "If I have been for a journey like that perhaps my brothers will believe that I am getting wise." So he arranged to meet the leopard at the lake shore next day, and bring with him three small parcels of food, which the leopard said would be needed.

The next morning they crossed over to the islands in a canoe, and near the landing-place was a big tree with a hole in it near the ground. "Put your three parcels in here," said the leopard, "for everyone who comes to these islands must pay tribute to Mukasa the wizard."

When they had walked some way the leopard sat down to rest and pulled some monkey-nuts out of his bag and began to eat. The poor hare had nothing, and the leopard only said: "Foolish people never look ahead–wise men are always prepared." A little farther on they came to a market, and the leopard called for banana beer, but when it was brought he said to the hare:

"This beer is full of dregs; I always drink banana beer through a straw; go and fetch one from the jungle near by." When the hare returned with the straw he found the leopard had drunk all the beer.

They walked on again until they came to the house where they were to spend the night, and the poor hare, hot and weary and hungry, lay down at once and was soon fast asleep.

Then the leopard crept out and stole a goat, and sprinkled some of the blood up the path to the house and smeared it on the paws of the hare, who was so sound asleep that he heard nothing.

In the early morning the owner of the goat found he had been robbed, and he followed the blood marks up to the house and found the little hare still sound asleep, all smeared and dirty, and he caught him and took him to the Island Council, and the chiefs said he was a cattle-stealer and must be killed.

The leopard went home much pleased, for he thought no one in the forest would know what he had done on the islands; but the forest is full of eyes and ears, and two weaver-birds who lived in a tree under his home had heard all his conversation with the hare, and they followed them to the islands and saw all that had happened, and came and told the five wise hares all about it. When the leopard returned the hares visited him and said:

"While you were away our young brother died and we are settling up his affairs and find that you owed him three goats."

The leopard was much annoyed, but he did not show it. He just said: "I keep all my goats on the islands where the pasture is very good; if one of you will come with me he shall choose three goats from my herd."

So one of the brothers went with him, and they arrived on the islands, and each put three parcels of food into the hollow tree for Mukasa the wizard.

In a little while the leopard sat down to rest and pulled out some monkey-nuts from his bag. The hare also began eating monkey-nuts, and said: "Wise men are always prepared; it is only foolish people who do not look ahead."

The leopard was very angry, but he did not show it, and they went on till they came to the market; but the hare cut a nice straw as they went through the jungle and hid it in his bag.

When the leopard called for banana beer the hare said politely: "Would you like a straw? Some people drink beer through a straw."

The leopard was almost too angry to speak, and they went on till they came to the house where they had arranged to spend the night. Then the hare took two bright polished cowrie shells and tied them over his eyes and lay down to sleep.

In the night the leopard crept out and stole a goat and sprinkled the blood on the path up to the house and went in, but he saw the gleaming white cowrie shells, and he thought they were the hare's eyes, and that he was still awake. So he waited and waited, and at last the day dawned, and the owner of the goat traced the blood marks up to the house and found the leopard all dirty and smeared, and took him to the Island Council, and the chiefs said he was a cattle-stealer and must be killed.

Then the wise hare returned to the forest and told his brothers all that had happened, and they thanked the weaver-birds for what they had done to help them in avenging their foolish young brother, and I never heard of another foolish hare from that time.

THE STORY OF THE COCK AND THE HEN

ONCE upon a time in the very old days the cock and the hen were jungle fowl, and did not know village life at all; they lived in the jungle and were feared by all the animals, because they had large red combs on their heads, and they said that these combs were full of fire.

Now all animals are very much afraid of fire, so the cock and the hen ruled the jungle, because if ever one of the animals displeased them they said: "If you do not do what I want I will burn you with my comb. Do you not see that it is red-hot?"

One day the old mother leopard came home and found that the fire in her kitchen had gone out, and she said to her little cub: "Run to the cock's house and ask him to give you a few glowing bits of charcoal to make our fire."

The cub went obediently, but he found the cock and the hen both sound asleep, and he was afraid to wake them.

The mother leopard said: "Take a little dry grass and creep up softly to the cock and light the grass from his comb." But the cub was afraid to go alone, so his mother went with him, and they crept up to the sleeping cock and hen and gently put the dry grass against their combs, but it did not light, and the grass was not even scorched, and the mother leopard put out her paw and touched them, and the combs were quite cold, although they looked red-hot.

Then she knew that the cock and hen had been telling lies all these years, and she roared with laughter and woke them up, and she said: "Now I know that you don't tell the truth; your combs are quite cold; there is no fire in them; the animals will not fear you any more; I am going to tell them all about it."

The cock and hen did not wait to hear what the jungle thought about it; they packed up their things and ran away to the village, and since that day they never returned to the jungle. They have always lived with men, and they like being safely shut up at night, for even now the leopards have not forgotten, and kill them if they find them out at night.

UGANDA LULLABY

SLEEP, little warrior, sleep,
  For the hares in the forest are sleeping,
    The Moon looks down from the skies;
    Brighter than Stars are thine eyes;
And thy mother her vigil is keeping.
    Sleep, little warrior, sleep.

Sleep, little chieftain, sleep,
  For soon the world will be waking
    And babyhood gone
    Like the verse of a song;
Thy mother's heart may be breaking.
    Sleep, little chieftain, sleep.

THE STORY OF THE TWO FRIENDS

ONCE upon a time there was a potter and his wife who had one child, a little boy, and as he grew older they were grieved to see that he was different from all other children.

He never played with them, or laughed, or sang; he just sat alone by himself, he hardly ever spoke to his parents, and he never learnt the nice polite manners of the other children in the village. He sat and thought all day, and no one knew what he thought about, and his parents were very sad.

The other women tried to comfort the potter's wife. They said: "Perhaps you will have another baby, and it will be like other children." But she said:

"I don't want another baby; I want this one to be nice." And the men of the village tried to cheer the potter. "Queer boys often become great men," they said. And one old man said: "Leave the boy alone; we shall see whether he is a wise man or a fool."

The potter went home and told his wife what the men had said, and the boy heard him, and it seemed to wake him up, and he thought it over for a few days, and at last one morning at dawn he took his stick in his hand and went into the forest to think there.

All day he wandered about, and at last he came to a little clearing on the side of a hill from which he could look down over the country. The Sun was setting over the distant blue hills, and everything was touched with a pink and golden light, and deep shadows lay on the banana gardens and forests in the distance, but the boy saw none of these things; he was footsore and weary and miserable, and he sat down on a fallen log, tired out with his long day. Suddenly a lion came out on to the clearing.

"What are you doing here all alone?" he said severely.

"I am very miserable," said the boy, "and I have come into the forest to think, for I do not know whether I am a wise man or a fool."

"Is that all you think about?" said the lion.

"Yes," answered the boy, "I think about it night and day."

"Then you are a fool," said the lion decidedly. "Wise men think about things that benefit the country." And he walked away.

An antelope came bounding out on the clearing and stopped to stare at the boy.

"What are you doing here?" he asked.

"I am very miserable," answered the boy; "I don't know whether I am a wise man or a fool."

"Do you ever eat anything?" said the antelope.

"Yes," said the boy, "my mother cooks twice a day, and I eat."

"Do you ever thank her?" said the antelope.

"No, I have never thought of that," answered the boy.

"Then you are a fool," said the antelope. "Wise men are always grateful." And he bounded off into the forest again.

Then a leopard came up and looked suspiciously at him.

"What are you doing here?" he asked crossly.

"I am very miserable," answered the boy; "I don't know if I am a wise man or a fool."

"Do they love you in your village?" asked the leopard.

"Am I a wise man or a fool?"
Asked the potter's son

"No, I don't think they do," said the boy. "I am not like other boys. I don't know them very well."

"Then you are a fool," said the leopard. "*All boys* are nice; I often wish *I* were a boy; wise men mix with their fellows and earn their respect." And he walked on sniffing.

Just then the big grey elephant came shuffling along the forest path, swinging his tail as he walked, and picking a twig here and a leaf there as he passed under the trees.

"What are you doing here all alone in the jungle when the Sun is setting?" he asked. "You should be at home in your village."

"I am very miserable," said the boy. "I don't know if I am a wise man or a fool."

"What work do you do?" asked the elephant.

"I don't do any work," said the boy.

"Then you are a fool," said the elephant. "All wise men work." And he swung away down the path which leads to the pool in the forest where the animals go to drink, and the boy put his head down in his hands and cried bitterly, as if his heart would break, for he did not know what to do.

After a little while he heard a gentle voice by his side: "My little brother, do not cry so; tell me your trouble." The boy raised his tear-stained face and saw a little hare standing by his side.

"I am very miserable," he said. "I am not like other people, and nobody loves me. I came into the forest to find out whether I am a wise man or a fool, and all the animals tell me I am a fool." And he put his head in his hands again and cried more bitterly than ever.

The hare let him cry on for a little while, and then he said: "My little brother, do not cry any more. What the animals have told you is true; they have told you to think great thoughts, to be grateful and kind to others, and, above all, to work. All these things are great and wise. The animals are never idle, and they marvel to see how men, with all their gifts, waste their lives. Think how surprised they are to see a boy like you, well and strong, doing nothing all day, for they know that the world is yours if you will make it so."

The King of the Snakes

The Sun had set behind the distant hills and the soft darkness was falling quickly over the forest, and the hare said: "Soon it will be chilly here; you are tired and hungry, and far from your village; come and spend the night in my home and we will talk of all these things."

So they went into the forest again, and the hare brought the boy water in a gourd and wonderful nuts to eat, and made him a soft bed of dry leaves.

And they talked of many things till the boy said: "My father is a potter, and I think I should like to be a potter too." "If you are, you must never be content with poor work," said the hare. "Your pottery must be the best in the country; never rest until you can make really beautiful things; no man has any right to send imperfect work out into the world." "Nobody will believe in me when I go home; they will think I am mad," said the boy. And the little hare answered: "Man's life is like a river, which flows always on and on; what is past is gone for ever, but there is clear water behind; no man can say it is too late, and you are only a boy with your life before you."

"They will laugh at me," said the boy.

"Wise men don't mind that," said the hare; "only fools are discouraged by laughter; you must prove to them that you are not a fool. I will teach you a song to sing at your work; it will encourage you:

> "When the shadows have melted in silver dawn,
> Farewell to my dreams of play.
> The forest is full of a waking throng,
> And the tree-tops ring with the birds' new song,
> And the flowers awake from their slumber long,
>   And the world is mine to-day.
>
> "My feet are sure and my hands are strong.
> Let me labour and toil while I may.
> When the Sun shall set in a sea of light,

And the shadows lengthen far into the night,
I shall take the rest which is mine by right,
For I'll win the world to-day."

In the early morning the hare went with the boy to the edge of the forest and they swore an oath of friendship, which is as sacred in the jungle as among men, and the hare said:

"Come back sometimes and see me, and we will spend a long day together in the forest. Come to this place and sing my song, and the birds will tell me you are there if I am too far away to hear."

So the boy went back to his village, and he found his mother digging in the garden, and he knelt down and greeted her as all nice Baganda children do, and he saw how pleased she was. Then he went to his father, and said: "I want to be a potter; teach me your work and I will try to learn it." And the potter was very much pleased to think that he would have a son to take on his trade after him, and all the people in the village heard and they rejoiced with the potter and his wife.

And the boy worked hard, and in after years he became a famous potter, and people came from all parts of the country to buy his pottery, for everyone knew that he never sold anything that was not beautiful and well made.

He made beautiful black pottery, and sometimes he put a design in white on it, and everything he made was good.

But sometimes the old black moods would return and he would feel sick of his work and all the people round him, and then he would go away at dawn to the edge of the forest and sing the hare's song, and the little hare would come running down the forest path, and the two friends would spend a long day together, while the man would shake out his heart and all its sorrows to the hare, and he never failed to get love and comfort and encouragement in return, and went back to his work full of hope.

This all happened many years ago; nowadays men think they are much wiser than the animals, but sometimes you may see a strange look in the eyes of an animal, as if it would say: "That man thinks he is wise, but he is only a fool." And the animals in the forests and jungles and in our houses watch everything we do, and they marvel when they see how some men waste their lives.

HOW THE GREY PARROTS GOT THEIR RED TAILS

ONCE upon a time there was a man and a woman who were very unhappy because they had no children. Their house was built, like all the houses in Uganda, in the middle of a banana garden, and the garden bordered on the caravan road.

In those days wicked people used to come to the country and steal men and women and children and take them away as slaves. Sometimes they stole them at night.

One day these slave-traders met a woman with a baby girl tied on her back, and they caught her and put her with the other slaves and drove them down the road; but they found the baby a great trouble, for it coughed all the time, so they left it in a banana garden by the roadside and went away across the borders of the country to the distant land, where they sold the people as slaves.

Now the garden happened to belong to the man and woman who wanted a child so much, and when the woman went out early in the morning to dig in her garden she found the baby, and ran and told her husband, and they rejoiced very much, and they took the little girl into their home, and she became like their own child, and called them father and mother, and because she had come to them in the early morning they called her Dawn.

They noticed at once that she had a curious little mark on her shoulder, like the footprint of a bird on the wet sand, but she was healthy and strong, and the cough soon went, and as she grew up the woman taught her how to keep a garden and how to cook the different kinds of bananas and vegetables and sauces and dried fish, and they were a very happy little family.

Near the house was a big tree of wild plums, and every season when the plums were ripe the boys from the village knocked them down with sticks and stones. But one day some parrots were in the tree, and a stone hit one of them and broke its leg, and although it managed to hold on with one claw to the branch, at last it was so exhausted that it fell to the ground. Dawn was near and saw it fall, and she saw how distressed the other parrots were, for they could not carry their brother home, and they were afraid that a wild cat might eat him if he slept out of doors all night.

So Dawn said: "Let me take care of him. My father and mother will soon make his leg well." So she took him home, and her father bound up the broken leg, and they gave him a nice place to roost in and some nuts and water, and he stayed with them till he was well.

The parrot had five brothers, and they came over from the islands every day to see him, and they and Dawn made great friends, and they told her many things about their life on the islands and the strange things they saw while they were flying over the country.

Now in those days parrots were quite grey, tails and all, and they told Dawn how much they would like to have red tails, for that is the heart's desire of every parrot; and the six parrots taught Dawn the recitation which every mother parrot teaches her children before they leave the nest:

> Never get up till the Sun gets up
> Or the mists will give you a cold.
> And a parrot whose lungs have once been touched,
> Will never live to be old.
>
> Never eat plums that are not quite ripe,
> For perhaps they will give you a pain;
> And never dispute what a hornbill says
> Or you'll never dispute again.
>
> Never despise the power of speech;
> Learn every word as it comes.
> For this is the pride of the parrot race,
> That they speak with a hundred tongues.

Never stay up when the Sun goes down,
But sleep in your own home bed,
And if you've been good, as a parrot should,
You will dream that your tail is red.

One day, while they were playing in the garden, a tortoise came up from his bed among the dry leaves and looked sleepily at them.

He was a very old tortoise, and he was very wise, for more than a hundred years he had said wise things to people, and everything he said came true. When he saw Dawn and the six grey parrots he said: "What is your greatest wish?" And Dawn said: "My greatest wish is to see the King, but we live so far from the capital I am afraid it will never be granted."

Then the parrots said: "Our greatest wish is to have red tails, for parrots love red more than any colour in the world; we should like tails like the sky at sunrise."

The old tortoise blinked his eyes at them for a minute or two, and then he said: "Dawn shall see the King, and all the parrots shall have red tails." And he went back into his bed of dry leaves and was soon fast asleep again.

Quite soon afterwards Dawn was standing by the big plum-tree on the road and the six parrots were chattering in the branches when two men passed. They were slave-traders, and when they saw Dawn was alone and no one was in sight, they thought they would steal her.

Dawn was so startled that they could easily have caught her, but the six parrots swooped down from the tree and attacked the men; they buried their claws in their hair, and pecked at their heads and ears and faces, and scratched them down their shoulders and arms, and Dawn shrieked, and the parrots screeched, and the men yelled with fright and pain, and people heard the noise and came running up.

Then Dawn told them what had happened, and they caught the two men and tied them with ropes and took them to the chief of the village. The next morning the chief heard the case, and he said: "I think these are the two men they are looking for in the capital. They must go before the King's Council, and the witnesses must go with them."

So Dawn and her father and mother and some of the people of the village and the six parrots set off for the capital.

When they arrived in the Council House they all knelt before the King, and the six parrots bowed low until their foreheads touched the ground; and Dawn hardly dared to lift her eyes.

When the King heard the case he said to the parrots: "You have saved this child's life. What reward can I give you?"

Then the six parrots bowed again till their foreheads touched the ground, and they said: "Oh, King, give us red tails, for that is the desire of every parrot's heart; give us tails like the sky at sunrise."

And the King said: "Your wish is granted. After the next moulting season your tails shall be red for ever and ever."

When the case was finished they all knelt again, and as Dawn bowed her head the King saw the little mark on her shoulder like a bird's footprint on the wet sand, and he asked:

"Who is this child?" And they told him her story.

Then the King sent for an old Princess who was his aunt, and when she came into the Council House he asked:

"Do you know this mark?" And she answered:

"It is the little lost Princess who disappeared with her nurse when they were going to the doctor to get some cough mixture many years ago."

Then the King took Dawn in his arms and said she must live with him always, and he allowed the man and the woman who had taken care of her and loved her so much to come and live with her too.

And when the next moulting season came the parrots lost their grey tail feathers and beautiful red ones grew in their place. And the six parrots who had earned this gift for their tribe were sent as ambassadors to thank the King, and as they bowed before him till their foreheads touched the ground, all the chiefs in the Council House saw their red tails and clapped their hands, for the colour was so beautiful, just like the sky at sunrise. Since that day all grey parrots have had red tails, and are very happy, and they love men and do what they can to help them, and even take the trouble to learn their language because the King gave them their heart's desire.

And the mother parrots added a verse to the recitation which they teach the children before they leave the nest:

> Always remember that man is your friend:
> Serve him and never tire.
> And be true to the King in everything,
> For he gave you your Heart's Desire.

Then Dawn told the King about the wise old tortoise, and they sent to fetch him, but the messengers couldn't wake him up, he was so fast asleep, and perhaps he is asleep still.

THE SONG OF THE OLD CARAVAN DAYS
(NALI NG'ENZE)

THORN bush and desert scrub,
  Rank grass and sand,
Stretches the wilderness
  On every hand.
Into the amber west
  Drops the red Sun;
Sudden the darkness falls,
  Whisp'ring of home.
Blue sparkling waters,
  Clear crystal streams,
Green sunny gardens,
  Land of my dreams.
By the camp-fire we sit,
  Sorrow and I.
God of the wilderness,
  Oh, let me die.

THE GUARDIANS OF THE SNAKES

THERE are still old people living in Uganda who remember the time when there were no white men in the country.

The first white men who came had to walk 800 miles from the coast, and the journey was very dangerous. They passed through many countries full of wild warlike tribes, over great plains and high mountains and swamps and rivers, and, finally, they had to cross the Great Lake in canoes; but when they arrived in Uganda they often lived there for many years without returning to England, and they learnt the customs of the Baganda and their language in a way which is impossible now that there are steamers and trains and so many white people that some of them never speak to the natives at all.

In 1895 two Englishmen were going home from Uganda. They had been six years in the country, and already they had seen many changes.

They crossed the Great Lake in canoes, and began the long march to Mombasa.

Day after day they marched with a long caravan of porters each with a load carried on his head, camping every night where there was fresh water, and sometimes doing double marches because the water was not good, and often watching the camp in turns by night when they were passing through the country of a warlike tribe or the big game countries where lions roared round the camp all night.

One day when the men were pitching the tents on the slope of an escarpment overlooking a vast plain the headman of the caravan said: "Near here lives an old prophet; he is very wise, and foretells the future, and everything that he says comes true."

The Englishmen were so interested that they decided to visit the old prophet, so when the heat of the day was over they set out, with the headman as their guide, to the prophet's hut on the hill-side. As they approached they saw the old man standing on a ledge of rock overlooking the plain, shading his eyes with his hands, and straining them to see something in the far distance.

When he saw the two Englishmen he uttered a great cry, and, trembling in every limb, he fell at their feet, gasping out:

"My dream! My dream! The Guardians of the Snakes!"

The white men spoke to him kindly. "Fear not," they said. "Tell us your dream."

Still trembling with excitement the old man began:

"My lords, I dreamt that I stood on that rock and looked out over the plain, and I saw a great encampment of people, and as I gazed I saw that they were guarding two great snakes that stretched away to the horizon, their scales glittering in the sunlight.

"When night fell I crept down the hill-side. Stealthily I threaded my way among the campfires and tents until I stood beside the two great snakes; then I stooped and touched them, and I was amazed, for they had no heads, they were hard and cold and made of iron.

"While I still wondered a man came and spoke to me. He was like you, my lords, his white skin was tanned with the Sun, and he spoke kindly to me.

"'Fear not,' he said. 'What are you doing here?'

"'My lord,' I answered, 'I am a poor man and have no wisdom; from my hut on the hill-top I saw this encampment and these two great snakes, and I came seeking to understand.'

"The man answered: 'I am the Guardian of the Snakes; they are the slaves of the white man; wherever he goes he takes them with him; they carry his women and children, his cattle and his goods, and wherever they arrive the old days fade away and new days come.

"'These slaves have come from the Great Sea, and they go to the Great Lake. They will change your country, and the old days will never return.'

"Then I woke up from my dream, but, my lords, it is ever present with me, and I spend my days restlessly looking towards the east, for I know that some day I shall see those two great snakes creeping through my country."

The two Englishmen looked out over the vast plain, and saw the native villages dotted here and there among their fields of grain–great herds of game grazing unmolested on the green slopes, vast untouched forests on the mountain-sides, and the long shadows thrown by the setting Sun lying on miles and miles of country where the foot of man had never trod, and they, too, wondered at the prophet's dream.

But some years afterwards one of them again stood on the ledge of rock and looked over the same plain, and saw farmsteads and fields and gardens, and the monotonous sound of sawmills rose from the forests and great herds of cattle grazed on the green slopes where once he had seen only antelope and zebra, and far in the distance two railway lines stretched away to the horizon, glittering like snakes' scales in the sunlight, and he remembered the old prophet and his dream.

Then he understood that the Guardian of the Snakes had spoken truly, for those snakes are the slaves of the white man–they carry his women and children, his cattle and his goods, and where they arrive the old days fade away and new days come. The old times never return, for the country is changed for ever.

PROVERBS

1. He who runs in the morning will tire before the day's march is over.

2. The monkey cannot be trusted to give a fair judgment on forest matters.

3. Do not call out for help before you need it.

4. He who has never had a sorrow cannot speak words of comfort.

5. Even a wise man does not know everything.

6. You can't dig with a spade handle, but it helps the spade to dig.

7. A dog knows his own business and his master's too.

8. Friendship is like a tailor's seam; it is the unpicking which causes trouble.

9. Splutter splutter isn't fire.

10. If you suffer in order to be beautiful don't blame anyone but yourself.

11. You never can tell if bananas are worth the trouble of making beer until you have done some of the work.

12. He who makes friends is wiser than he who quarrels.

13. Never give advice to an enemy.

14. Caution is not cowardice: even the ants march armed.

15. He who goes slowly goes far.

16. It is no good asking the spirits to help you run if you don't mean to sprint.

17. No man fears what he has seen grow.

18. He who says others are swindling will not lend you anything.

19. Beer isn't food: don't be content with it.

20. He who has two homes never gets a meal.

21. The champion who has thrown his opponent says: "That is enough."

22. You can't tell the age of a beardless man, or the time on a cloudy day.

23. What the herd will stand the cowherd will put up with.

24. Let me die for something worth while.

25. The grumbler does not leave his job, but he discourages possible applicants.

26. The iron fears the blacksmith.

27. A man who is always being slandered is like a knife constantly in use–no one has time to polish it.

28. Lazy people always set others to work.

29. Everyone has his own tastes.

30. Wait until you are grown up before you try to jump as far as your father.

CPSIA information can be obtained
at www.ICGtesting.com
Printed in the USA
LVHW030435310522
720054LV00001B/79